Chri

D1539388

Roadmap to Success:

Briefing Managers about Affirmative Action Results
– An HR Professional's Guide

By

Thomas H. Nail

Cornelia Gamlem, SPHR

Cover designed by: Erik Gamlem
Big Heavy Design
www.bigheavydesign.com

Roadmap to Success:

Briefing Managers about Affirmative Action Results – An HR Professional's Guide

Thomas H. Nail
President
THOMAS HOUSTON associates, inc.
620 Herndon Parkway, Suite 200
Herndon, VA   20170
(703) 481-9839
e-mail: tom.nail@thomashouston.com
web-site: www.thomashouston.com

Cornelia Gamlem, SPHR
President
GEMS Group ltd
P. O. Box 148
Herndon, VA   20172
(703) 709-9114
e-mail: cornelia@gemsgroup-hr.com
web-site: www.gemsgroup-hr.com

Roadmap to Success: Briefing Managers about Affirmative Action Results – An HR Professional's Guide (Roadmap) is published only as an informational guide. The reader should keep in mind that although this *Roadmap* is designed to provide accurate and current information on employment law compliance issues as of the date of publication, the information contained herein is general in nature and is not intended to be relied upon as legal advice. The resolution of each circumstance encountered by readers of this *Roadmap* would ultimately be determined on a case-by-case basis, depending upon the particular facts presented, and legal counsel should also be consulted as appropriate. THOMAS HOUSTON associates, inc. and GEMS Group ltd welcomes the opportunity to discuss in greater detail the information set forth in this book and how it might apply to the specific needs of your company.

DEDICATION

This book is dedicated to our spouses,
Candyce Nail and Carl Gamlem, and our sons,
Alex and Christopher Nail and Erik Gamlem
who share our "road trips" and "life
journeys".

TABLE OF CONTENTS

PREFACE

HOW TO USE THIS MANAGEMENT BRIEFING

The **Introduction for Human Resource Professionals** provides guidance and instructions on the contents of this sample briefing and how to use it to communicate affirmative action program results to the company's management staff.

Affirmative Action Program Compliance Background is a briefing paper that can be distributed to the company's executive team and/or management staff.

The **Management Briefing – Introduction** provides an overview of the regulations and requirements. The information in this section can be incorporated as points in a presentation when communicating this information in that format.

Comparing Incumbency to Availability – Determining Underutilization explains the process of comparing workforce composition to availability to determine if the company's workforce is representative of the individuals with the skills and talents in the market, with respect to gender, race, and ethnicity. This section also explains placement rate goals and provides sample formats to present the data to the management staff.

Accomplishment of Past Year Goals examines the company's current situation with respect to goals set in the prior year Affirmative Action Plan and where good faith efforts have helped to meet those goals or improve in areas where job groups were underutilized. Sample formats are also provided.

Impact Ratio Analysis explains the types of potential problems this analysis can uncover and the follow-up action required to determine if employment decisions were made in a nondiscriminatory manner. It also provides a sample approach for presenting the results to management.

Evaluation of Organizational Units explains the types of potential problems this analysis can uncover and the follow-up action required to determine if minorities or females are being steered into positions with limited opportunities.

Compensation explains the importance of conducting a pay equity analysis.

INTRODUCTION
FOR HUMAN RESOURCE
PROFESSIONALS

This product was developed to assist Human Resource Professionals:

- Understand the purpose and intent of affirmative action as it relates to line managers
- Realize the importance of line management responsibility for equal employment opportunity/affirmative action
- Design a briefing of the results of the company's affirmative action program for presentation to management staff
- Design a briefing containing periodic progress of accomplishments of affirmative action goals

Sample charts are included for illustrative purposes along with blank tables that will assist in the customization of affirmative action program results.

There are instructions on customizing the material contained in this document. The instructions are distinguished by the use of Century Gothic text, like the text used here. Additionally, sample, illustrative language is presented in Century Gothic text.

This briefing may be made available to management in a number of formats. For example, the material in this document may be combined with affirmative action program results to develop a slide presentation. A customized briefing paper may be distributed to supplement the presentation.

Distribution should be made to management staff only. Prudent practice is that affirmative action data is only provided to management staff on a "need-to-know" basis. Keep in mind that this data is considered to be confidential and it may have implications on manpower or staffing trends. It is for these reasons that it is advised to limit the number of people who receive this information and the manner in which it is distributed. It is not recommended to make it available on a company intranet. If the information is made available to employees outside of the management staff who have a need to know, it could be difficult to protect the confidentiality of the data, and the company could suffer negative repercussions at a later time.

AFFIRMATIVE ACTION PROGRAM COMPLIANCE: BACKGROUND

Companies that receive contracts or subcontracts from the federal government are required to develop affirmative action programs to comply with the regulations that support three separate federal laws. All three of these laws prohibit employment discrimination and require contractors to exercise good faith efforts so that members of certain protected classes have the opportunity to be hired and advanced in employment. Together these laws are known as the Federal Contract Compliance Program. Executive Order 11246 prohibits discrimination on the basis of race, color, religion, gender, or national origin. The Rehabilitation Act of 1973 prohibits discrimination on the basis of disability, and the Vietnam Era Veterans' Readjustment Assistance Act of 1974 (VEVRAA) prohibits discrimination against certain classes of veterans.

The Federal Contract Compliance Program has three requirements. First, it prohibits discrimination against anyone on the basis of race, color, religion, gender, national origin, disability, or veteran status. Second, it requires contractors to engage in specific activities to ensure that employees and applicants are treated without regard to their race, color, religion, gender, national origin, disability, or veteran status. Both requirements are applicable during the hiring process as well as during the employment relationship. Finally, it requires a formal documented plan (Affirmative Action Plan) for each of the contractor's establishments or functional lines of business. Accompanying each of these laws is a specific set of regulations that describe the required components of affirmative action programs. These regulations are codified in the federal regulations at 41 CFR Chapter 60 and are legally binding.

An Affirmative Action Plan (AAP) describes a company's programs, policies, and practices designed to ensure that all individuals have equal opportunities in all employment decisions and practices. It also contains the results of several statistical analyses of the company's workforce and employment practices for the prior year. The purpose of these analyses is to identify areas of a workforce where qualified members of protected groups are not fully represented, as well as possible discriminatory practices. An AAP also describes corrective action to be taken when deficiencies are found. It is a temporary document that must be updated each year.

The Department of Labor's Office of Federal Contract Compliance Programs (OFCCP) is the agency with authority to enforce these laws by auditing a company's AAP and employment practices. If, as the result of an audit, the OFCCP finds that a company is not in compliance with the regulations, it will issue a Notice of Violation and attempt voluntary settlement through a Conciliation Agreement. If a voluntary settlement cannot be reached, the agency can move to impose sanctions and penalties including withholding contract payments, cancellation or termination of existing federal contracts, or debarring the company from receipt of any future federal contracts or subcontracts.

Affirmative Action Plan

An Affirmative Action Plan is a management tool that documents a company's on-going efforts including the results of certain quantitative analyses. This plan or "tool" is designed to assist in affirmative action efforts, and it should be used in a diagnostic manner to enhance a company's commitment to EEO/affirmative action.

The plan must be updated annually; writing the plan is an event.

Affirmative Action Program

An affirmative action program is a company's effort to ensure equal employment opportunity within its employment and human resources policies, practices and processes. It institutionalizes a company's commitment to affirmative action. The OFCCP expects that it is part of the way that a company regularly conducts its business.

The program is the way in which a company conducts business; it is a process rather than an event.

MANAGEMENT BRIEFING: INTRODUCTION

Affirmative action program compliance is measured and judged against two sets of standards – qualitative and quantitative – which are set forth in the federal regulations at 41 CFR 60-2.35.

The first standard is the company's compliance with the affirmative action obligations, which is measured by the company's efforts to identify equal employment opportunity problems and take appropriate corrective action. These are the qualitative standards. During an audit, the OFCCP will focus its resources on the action undertaken to promote equal employment opportunity, rather than merely on technical compliance.

Affirmative action compliance is measured by the *nature and extent* of activities under **41 CFR §60-2.17**, identifying problem areas and implementing appropriate action-oriented programs to address the problems. The requirements include:

A. Designation of Responsibility - 41 CFR §60-2.17 (a)

- An individual named as EEO Officer or Coordinator who has

    - the authority, resources, support, and access to top management to ensure the effective implementation of the affirmative action program

    - the responsibility for implementing the affirmative action program

    - the responsibility for ensuring that policies and practices supporting the program are properly executed

B. Identification of Problem Areas – 41 CFR §60-2.17 (b)

- An in-depth analysis of the total employment process to identify impediments to EEO
- An evaluation of
    - workforce by organizational unit and job group
    - personnel activity
    - selection, recruitment, referral, and other personnel procedures
    - compensation systems
    - any other areas that might impact success of the affirmative action program

C. Action-Oriented Programs – 41 CFR §60-2.17 (c)

- Designed to
    - correct any problem areas identified in the §60-2.17(b) process
    - attain established goals and objectives
- Demonstrate good faith efforts beyond procedures which have produced inadequate results in the past to
    - remove identified barriers
    - expand employment opportunities
    - produce measurable results

6

D. Internal Audit & Reporting – 41 CFR § 60-2.17 (d)

- Designed to periodically measure effectiveness of the total affirmative action program
- Include the following four key actions:
  - *Monitor* records of all personnel activity
  - Require scheduled internal *reporting*
  - *Review* reports with all levels of management
  - *Advise* top management and submit recommendations

The second standard is the company's compliance with its nondiscrimination obligations. This is determined by the analysis of statistical data and other non-statistical information which would indicate whether employees and applicants are being treated without regard to their race, color, religion, gender, or national origin.

Everyone shares responsibility for nondiscrimination compliance as well as the success of the affirmative action program. All employment decisions made (e.g. hires, promotions, terminations, compensation, and discipline) are subject to scrutiny by government auditors. For this reason, it is important that during the hiring and promotion process, for example, all candidates are evaluated against the requirements of open positions. When making decisions to terminate an employee, it is important to follow company policy regarding workplace conduct, discipline, and performance. **(Note:** You can provide more specific information about company policies here.)

This briefing focuses on nondiscrimination standards and the results of quantitative analysis.

COMPARING INCUMBENCY TO AVAILABILITY: DETERMINING UNDERUTILIZATION

Federal contractors are required to compare the percentage of minorities and females in each job group with the availability determined for those job groups. A job group combines job titles based on similarity of job content, pay rates, and opportunities for advancement. Where the percentage of minorities or females employed in a particular job group is less than would reasonably be expected given their availability percentage in that particular job group, placement rate goals are established in the Affirmative Action Plan. Underutilization identifies those areas where the representation of minorities and/or females is less than reasonably expected.

The **Job Group Analysis Summary** displays the total number and percentage (workforce representation) of minorities and females within each of the company's job groups.

The **Incumbency v. Availability** table contains the workforce representation, the availability, and a declaration of underutilization for each of the company's job groups.

For those job groups where incumbency is less than availability, placement rate goals are set. (See **Annual Placement Goals** table.) Placement rate goals represent a commitment to place minorities and females into job groups at the rate at which they are available. These goals are process goals versus final destinations for job group composition. Placement rate goals do not represent quotas. **Quotas are expressly forbidden.**

9

What are Placement Rate Goals?

Simply stated, a placement rate goal means that for however many opportunities there are to place employees into that job group, some percentage of those placements will be minorities and females. That percentage is equal to the availability rate for minorities and females.

- These goals are established for those job groups determined to be underutilized.

- Their purpose is to eliminate underutilization.

- They are maintained as long as underutilization exists in the job group.

- They are established when a job group is underutilized by more than one whole person.

- They must be updated annually.

- Separate goals must be established for minorities and females.

- Once a goal is set, good faith efforts must be exercised to accomplish the goal.

- A placement rate goal is the annual rate at which minorities and females are placed in an underutilized job group.

- A placement rate goal is the availability percentage for minorities and females.

- A placement rate goal is a target, not a quota.

- Placement rate goals are expressed as a percentage placement rate rather than numerical.

    What's the difference? The rate at which something is done is different from the number of times it is done.

10

SAMPLE COMPANY NAME

JOB GROUP ANALYSIS SUMMARY

Job Group		Total Number in Job Group	Total Number of Females	Total Percentage of Females	Total Number of Minorities	Total Percentage of Minorities
1A	Executives	18	3	16.67%	1	5.56%
1B	Managers	26	8	30.77%	4	15.38%
1C	Technical Supervisors	6	2	33.33%	0	
1D	Administrative Supv.	13	5	38.46%	4	30.77%
2A	Technical Professional	64	16	25.00%	11	17.19%
2B	Administrative Professionals	44	27	61.36%	15	34.09%
4A	Sales Professionals	7	2	28.57%	1	14.29%
5A	Administrative Support	16	15	93.75%	11	68.75%
5B	Clerical Support	12	10	83.33%	6	50.00%

Instruction: This is a sample form, included for illustration purposes only. In preparing this information to present to your management, you can use this form or a similar format. A blank form is included on the next page if you wish to use it.

You should consult the Job Group Analysis in your completed Affirmative Action Plan to obtain the information about your company's workforce for this summary.

11

YOUR COMPANY NAME

JOB GROUP ANALYSIS SUMMARY

Job Group	Total Number in Job Group	Total Number of Females	Total Percentage of Females	Total Number of Minorities	Total Percentage of Minorities

SAMPLE COMPANY NAME

INCUMBENCY v. AVAILABILITY

Job Group	Total Number in Job Group*	Total Number of Incumbents* Females/ Minorities	Total Percentage of Incumbents* Females/ Minorities	Percentage Availability** Females/ Minorities	Under-utilized? ***
1A Executives	18	3	16.67%	21.22%	Yes
		1	5.56%	21.00%	Yes
1B Managers	26	8	30.77%	19.29%	
		4	15.38%	21.37%	Yes
1C Technical Supervisors	6	2	33.33%	24.75%	
		0	0%	12.36%	Yes
1D Administrative Supv.	13	5	38.46%	35.82%	
		4	30.77%	28.24%	
2A Technical Professional	64	16	25.00%	31.06%	
		11	17.19%	22.65%	Yes
2B Administrative Professionals	44	27	61.36%	58.42%	
		15	34.09%	34.54%	
4A Sales Professionals	7	2	28.57%	39.35%	
		1	14.29%	18.21%	
5A Administrative Support	16	15	93.75%	57.01%	
		11	68.75%	37.33%	
5B Clerical Support	12	10	83.33%	77.70%	
		6	50.00%	42.975	

Instruction: This is a sample form, included for illustration purposes only. In preparing this information to present to your management, you can use this form or a similar format. A blank form is included on the next page if you wish to use it.

* You should consult the Job Group Analysis in your completed Affirmative Action Plan to obtain this information.

** You should consult the Availability Analysis in your completed Affirmative Action Plan to obtain this information.

*** Underutilization can be determined by conducting any number of statistical methodologies. You should consult the analysis in your completed Affirmative Action Plan to obtain this information.

YOUR COMPANY NAME

INCUMBENCY v. AVAILABILITY

Job Group	Total Number in Job Group	Total Incumbents Females/ Minorities	Total Percentage of Incumbents Females/ Minorities	Percentage Availability Females/ Minorities	Under-utilized?

SAMPLE COMPANY NAME

ANNUAL PLACEMENT GOALS

Job Group	Placement Goal Females*	Placement Goal Minorities*
1A Executives	21.22%	21.00%
1B Managers		21.37%
1C Technical Supervisors		12.36%
1D Administrative Supv.		
2A Technical Professional		22.65%
2B Administrative Professionals		
4A Sales Professionals		
5A Administrative Support		
5B Clerical Support		

Instruction: This is a sample form, included for illustration purposes only. In preparing this information to present to your management, you can use this form or a similar format. A blank form is included on the next page if you wish to use it.

* You should consult the Annual Placement Goals chart in your completed Affirmative Action Plan to obtain this information.

16

YOUR COMPANY NAME

ANNUAL PLACEMENT GOALS

Job Group	Placement Goal Females	Placement Goal Minorities

ACCOMPLISHMENT OF PAST YEAR'S GOALS

The progress made against goals set in the prior Affirmative Action Plan year must be evaluated. This is accomplished by examining the actual placements of protected classes into those job groups that were underutilized and comparing that placement rate to the prior year goals.

Placements include external and internal placements. External placements include new hires as well as offers made but declined because employment declinations represent positive efforts to meet the established goals. Internal placements include those employees who changed job groups through promotion or other employment activity where a selection decision was made.

The Goals Accomplishment Report displays the results of affirmative action efforts toward achieving those goals that were established for the time-period covered by the prior year Affirmative Action Plan.

Note: In addition to providing a briefing on the Goals Accomplishment for the prior year Affirmative Action Plan, line management can be provided with progress reports **throughout** the year (e.g. quarterly or semi-annually) using the same tables presented here.

SAMPLE COMPANY NAME

GOAL ACCOMPLISHMENT REPORT

Job Group	Total Placements [1]	Females			Minorities		
		Goal % [2]	Placement Number/ Percentage [3]	Goal Met? [4]	Goal % [5]	Placement Number/ Percentage [6]	Goal Met? [7]
1A Executives	9	21.22%	2 22.22%	Yes	18.31%	1 11.11%	No
1B Managers	12	19.31%	5 41.67%	Yes	20.29%	3 25.00%	Yes
1C Technical Supervisors	4				23.67%	0	No
1D Administrative Supervisors	7	41.97%	2 28.57%	No			
2A Technical Professional	23				22.65%	5 21.74%	Yes

---

[1] Represents the number of placements into this job group during the past year. This can be New Hires, Transfers into the AAP from another one of your company's AAPs, Promotions into this job group from another job group, Reclassifications, or other internal movements into this job group from another job group.

[2] Represents the placement rate goal that was set for females in your prior year AAP. You must consult your prior year AAP for this information.

[3] Represents the number of females placed into the job group during the prior 12 months and the percentage (e.g. 2/9 = 22.22%) of female placements.

[4] If the percentage of placements exceeds the goal, then you can declare that the goal was met.

[5] Represents the placement rate goal that was set for minorities in your prior year AAP. You must consult your prior year AAP for this information.

[6] Represents the number of minorities placed into the job group during the prior 12 months and the percentage (e.g. 1/9 = 11.11%) of minority placements.

[7] If the percentage of placements does not exceed the goal, then you must declare that the goal was not met.

The form on the next page is a sample form, included for illustration purposes only. In preparing this information to present to your management, you can use this form or a similar format. A blank form is included on the next page if you wish to use it.

You only need to show those job groups that were underutilized in the prior year AAP.

YOUR COMPANY NAME

GOAL ACCOMPLISHMENT REPORT

Job Group	Total Placements	Females			Minorities		
		Goal %	Placement Number/ Percentage	Goal Met?	Goal %	Placement Number/ Percentage	Goal Met?

IMPACT RATIO ANALYSIS

The Impact Ratio Analysis (IRA) is performed to determine if any adverse impact exists for minorities or females with respect to their selection for hire, promotion, termination, or any other employment practice. Adverse impact is an indicator of potential discrimination toward individuals within protected groups. If adverse impact is determined in any element of the selection process or within specific employment practices, then all selection procedures and employment practices should be investigated for discriminatory elements. The IRA compares the selection rate of the protected group with the selection rate of the non-protected group.

Statistically significant adverse impact (as determined by applying the Standard Deviation Test) is an indicator of potential discrimination and requires identification of why adverse impact exists in the specific employment practice. Where selection decisions are not able to be explained, the company is potentially liable for allegations of discrimination and can incur financial liability. While the Department of Labor cannot impose fines, make whole relief including back pay and interest for up to two years can be granted to those individuals deemed to be adversely affected by the discriminatory practices. If it is determined that the discrimination was willful, then affected individuals could be granted three years of back pay.

- The IRA serves to identify possible problem areas where the selection rate for minorities or females is less than 80% of the selection rate for non-minorities or males for positive employment actions (hiring, promotions and training).

- The IRA serves to identify possible problem areas where the selection rate for minorities or females is greater than 120% of the selection rate for non-minorities or males for negative employment actions (terminations and layoffs).

- Situations where apparent adverse impact exists must be investigated to identify potential problem areas.

- Any problem areas found as a result of such investigation must be explained or resolved with documented evidence.

- Written justification for each selection decision that caused apparent adverse impact and documented evidence of actions taken to resolve actual or apparent adverse impact must be available for review by Department of Labor compliance officers.

The Impact Ratio Analysis compares (by gender and race) Hires to Applicants, Offers to Applicants, Promotions to Incumbents, and Terminations to Incumbents. The comparisons are done for each job group.

The following is a discussion of the results of the *SAMPLE COMPANY* Impact Ratio Analysis.

Hires vs. Applicants:

There was no significant disparity in hiring decisions in any of the job groups for minorities or females.

Job Group 2A had adverse impact with respect to females under the 80% rule. However, when the Standard Deviation test was applied, it appeared to be occurring by chance.

Promotions vs. Incumbents:

There was no significant disparity in promotion decisions in any of the job groups for minorities or females.

Job Group 2A had adverse impact with respect to minorities under the 80% rule. However, when the Standard Deviation test was applied, it appeared to be occurring by chance.

Involuntary Terminations vs. Incumbents:

There was no significant disparity in termination decisions in any of the job groups for females.

A significant disparity was noted in Job Group 2A with respect to minorities. All involuntary termination decisions in this job group were reviewed. This review showed that all terminations were appropriately documented and conducted in accordance with our company policy.

Layoffs vs. Incumbents:

Layoffs were analyzed separately from other types of Involuntary Terminations. There was no indication of adverse impact for layoffs in any job group.

Note to HR: The following is an alternate way of displaying for managers the results of the *SAMPLE COMPANY* IMPACT RATIO ANALYSIS in a chart format.

Action	Adverse Impact	Job Group
Hires vs. Applicants	Yes	**Females:** 2A –Technical Professionals*
Promotions vs. Incumbents	Yes	**Minorities** . 2A –Technical Professionals*
Involuntary Terminations vs. Incumbents	Yes	**Minorities** 2A –Technical Professionals**
Layoffs Terminations vs. Incumbents	No	

* Adverse Impact under the 80% rule

** Statistically Significant Adverse Impact

26

EVALUATION OF ORGANIZATIONAL UNITS

An evaluation of the workforce by organizational unit must be conducted to determine any potential barriers to equal employment opportunity. (**Note:** You should explain the organizational units for your company, such as department, division, or some other unit.) The ideal is that minorities and females should be distributed throughout the workforce in an equitable manner. A high percentage or concentration of females or minorities in a particular unit **could** be an indicator of "steering" individuals into positions that traditionally have limited opportunity for advancement. Conversely, an under-representation of females or minorities **could** be an indicator of potential barriers or "glass walls." This evaluation must be performed annually as part of the affirmative action program.

Note: You should explain the methodology your company uses to complete this evaluation and present the results of the analysis you conducted. You should advise your managers that the results of this evaluation provide direction for future affirmative action efforts.

Example: The JAAR Analysis is one method of evaluating the workforce by organizational units (e.g. departments). The JAAR (Job Area Acceptance Range) Analysis compares the company's total workforce contained in the Affirmative Action Plan to an individual segment of that workforce. The individual segment may be a department or any organizational unit selected to be analyzed. The idea is that the distribution of females and minorities in the individual segment should be similar to that of the distribution of females and minorities in the total workforce.

27

COMPENSATION

Compensation analysis, or pay equity, has become an extremely important issue in recent OFCCP compliance evaluations. Companies are prohibited from discriminating in their compensation practices and an analysis of compensation systems is required under **41 CFR §60-2.17(b)(3)**. Compensation issues must be addressed in detail in preparation for an OFCCP compliance review.

Instances where minorities and/or females are paid less than non-minorities and/or males who are performing the same or substantially the same jobs must be analyzed. Pay practices must also be examined. More than likely, there will be situations where some degree of disparity exists. This is not, however, an indication that discrimination necessarily exists. There may be several bona fide, job-related reasons for a difference in pay between individuals. For example:

- Education
- Total work experience
- Seniority
- Time in job
- Performance
- Specialized job knowledge
- Specialized training
- Reassignment without pay reduction, red circling
- Company acquisitions, mergers, or restructuring
- Geographic location

When pay disparities are identified, it is important to examine each situation and determine if the disparity is due to bona fide, job-related reasons. If bona fide, job-related reasons cannot be identified and supported, then a presumption of discrimination will exist. The examples listed above are some of the legitimate, nondiscriminatory reasons for pay differences. This list is not intended to be all-inclusive and there may be additional explanations.

Note: You can explain the methodology your company uses to complete this evaluation. You should present the results of the analysis to your management or otherwise advise them of identified problem areas. A meaningful analysis of the pay practices and identification of any apparent disparity may be completed by following the Cohort Analysis procedure. In analyzing a large workforce, it may be helpful to use an electronic spreadsheet application.

Index

.

About the Authors

Thomas H. Nail is the President and founder of THOMAS HOUSTON associates, inc., a human resource management consultancy, which he began in 1978. The firm, whose core business is in equal employment opportunity and affirmative action, serves a nationwide client base from its offices in metropolitan Washington, DC and Fort Lauderdale, Florida.

A graduate of the University of Buffalo, Mr. Nail has been in the human resource field for over thirty years. Since writing his first affirmative action plan in the early 1970's, Mr. Nail and his staff have completed over 7,000 plans for clients in a multitude of industries in both the private and public sectors. He has directed over 450 OFCCP compliance reviews throughout the United States.

A longtime member of the Society for Human Resource Management (SHRM), Mr. Nail served on SHRM's Workplace Diversity Committee from 1981 to 2000. He assisted in the development and publication of SHRM's *Equal Employment Opportunity Manual for Managers and Supervisors* and has authored numerous articles and white papers for SHRM publications. In addition, Mr. Nail is the author of *Succeeding with Affirmative Action: A Comprehensive Desk Resource for Managers.* As a member of the Office of Federal Contract Compliance Program's National Liaison Committee, he assisted in writing the *OFCCP Federal Contract Compliance Manual.* He is frequently interviewed and quoted in national human resources publications.

Cornelia Gamlem, SPHR is President and founder of the GEMS Group ltd, a Human Resources consulting firm. She has over 20 years in the Human Resource Profession and worked for a Fortune 500 IT firm where she was responsible for managing policies, programs, and initiatives supporting best human resources and employment practices. Ms. Gamlem served on national task forces focused on issues of equal employment opportunity, affirmative action, and workplace diversity. Since starting her practice, she has consulted with a wide range of clients on these issues.

A graduate of Marymount University, where she received a Masters Degree in Human Resource Management, Ms. Gamlem is also certified as Senior Professional in Human Resources (SPHR).

An active volunteer with the Society for Human Resource Management (SHRM), Ms. Gamlem has served on its National Board of Directors, its Global Forum Board of Directors, and chaired its National Workplace Diversity Committee. She has authored articles and white papers for SHRM and industry publications. Ms. Gamlem has presented at SHRM conferences, the American Bar Association and other business groups, and has been interviewed by *The New York Times, Financial Times, Newsday,* and *Fortune.* She teaches at George Mason University, Trinity College, and Mary Washington College.

Other Books By These Authors

Roadmap to Success: 5 Steps to Putting Action into your Affirmative Action Program by Thomas H. Nail and Cornelia Gamlem

The first in the *Roadmap* series is a comprehensive guide through the required elements of affirmative action program implementation. It provides practical guidance on those activities that support a commitment to equal employment opportunity and non-discrimination. The 5-step process includes a Review of The Basics of Affirmative Action, Understanding the Regulations, Evaluating the Results of the Quantitative Analyses, Conducting the Qualitative Analyses, and Developing a Program for Individuals with Disabilities and Veterans. It incorporates checklists and key observation points for self-evaluation and appendices with expanded information on required analyses as well as a comprehensive outreach and recruitment directory for maximizing good faith efforts.

Succeeding with Affirmative Action: A Comprehensive Desk Resource for Managers by Thomas H. Nail

This resource manual provides easy to understand information and answers about the entire affirmative action compliance process. Each topic contains a detailed introduction, followed by "Key Points to Remember," and concludes with a "Checklist of Audit Points." The desk resource contains copies of the applicable laws and regulations as well as sample forms and letters used during the compliance process.

Visit Us On The Web

THOMAS HOUSTON associates, inc.
www.thomashouton.com

GEMS Group ltd
www.gemsgroup-hr.com